Bob Chilcott

Furusato　故郷

5 UPPER-VOICE ARRANGEMENTS OF JAPANESE SONGS

日本の歌による５つの合唱曲（高声合唱用）

MUSIC DEPARTMENT

OXFORD

UNIVERSITY PRESS

OXFORD
UNIVERSITY PRESS

Great Clarendon Street, Oxford OX2 6DP,
United Kingdom

Oxford University Press is a department of the University of Oxford.
It furthers the University's aim of excellence in research, scholarship,
and education by publishing worldwide

Oxford is a registered trade mark of Oxford University Press
in the UK and in certain other countries

Impression: 7

ISBN 978-0-19-339082-9

Music origination by Enigma Music Production Services, Amersham, Bucks.
Printed in Great Britain on acid-free paper by
Halstan & Co. Ltd, Amersham, Bucks.

Japanese translations by Miyako Hashimoto

Contents

Composer's Note

I have been very fortunate to come into contact with the fine and flourishing choral life of Japan through a number of visits to the country under the auspices of the Japan Choral Association. A very warm and happy relationship has also developed with Keiichi Asai and the Kyoto Echo Choir, and it is to them that I affectionately dedicate this set of arrangements of Japanese songs. I am very grateful to those at Pana Musica in Kyoto who suggested the selection of songs and to the poet Charles Bennett, who wrote the English singing translations. Thanks are also due to Tsuyoshi Chiba and to my friend from student days in London, Miyako Hashimoto, at whose suggestion I have dedicated the song 'Furusato' to the victims of the devastating Japanese earthquake of March 2011. The original mixed-voice edition of this collection was published in 2011, and I made this version in March 2012 for a workshop I gave in Kyoto for women's choirs.

BOB CHILCOTT

日本合唱連盟との幸運な繋がりの下に幾度かに渡る来日を重ねる中で、日本の大変優れた、そして活発なコーラス界との関係を深めて来れたことを大変幸せに思います。この合唱曲集は、これまで友情を温め合って来た「合唱団京都エコー」と浅井敬壹さんに捧げます。曲目の選定についてご提案頂いたパナムジカ様と、英語の歌詞の作詞者のチャールズ・ベネットさんに心より感謝いたします。更に、出版に当たってお手伝い頂いた千葉剛さん及び学生時代よりの旧友の橋本美弥子さんにも、感謝の意を表させて頂きます。尚、橋本さんのご提案により、「故郷」の歌を2011年3月の悲惨な東北震災の被災者の方々に捧げることにいたしました。オリジナルの混声合唱版は2011年に出版され、この高声用の編曲は2012年に京都で行った女声合唱のワークショップのために書きました。

ボブ・チルコット

Sunayama
砂山

Hakushu Kitahara (1885–1942)
English version by
Charles Bennett (b. 1954)

SHINPEI NAKAYAMA (1887–1952)
arr. BOB CHILCOTT (b. 1955)

1. う みは あら う み　むこうは さ ー どーよ
1. Waves on the sand are＿ fall - ing,　fall - ing＿ from the　eve - ning sky.

すずめなーけーな け　もうひは くーれた
Spar-rows are shreds of＿ dark - ness;　dark - ness＿ flies on　fea-thers of night.

Mura Matsuri
村祭

English version by
Charles Bennett (b. 1954)

Trad. Japanese
arr. BOB CHILCOTT (b. 1955)

ドン ドン ヒャ ラ ラ ドン ヒャ ラ ラ あ さ か ら き こ え る
don don hya-la-la, don hya-la-la. Drum-ming in the ce-le-bra-tion,

ふ え た い こ
pi-ping in the joy!

2. と し も ほ う ね ん ま ん さ く で
2. We are the har-vest on the spread-ing vil-lage tree,

3. みのりのあーきに
3. We are ev - er thank-ful for the

かみさまの　　めぐみたたえるむらまつり
pro-mise of the year,　Pour-ing your bless-ings on the peo-ple of the land.

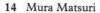

ドン ドン ヒャ ラ ラ　ドン ヒャ ラ ラ　　ドン ドン ヒャ ラ ラ　ドン ヒャ ラ ラ
Don don hya - la - la,　don hya - la - la,　　don don hya - la - la,　don hya - la - la.

き い て も　こ こ ろ が い さ み た つ　　　い さ み た つ
Drum-ming in the　ce - le - bra-tion, pi-ping in the joy!　　pi-ping in the joy!

Oborozukiyo
おぼろ月夜

Tatsuyuki Takano (1876–1947)
English version by
Charles Bennett (b. 1954)

TEIICHI OKANO (1878–1941)
arr. BOB CHILCOTT (b. 1955)

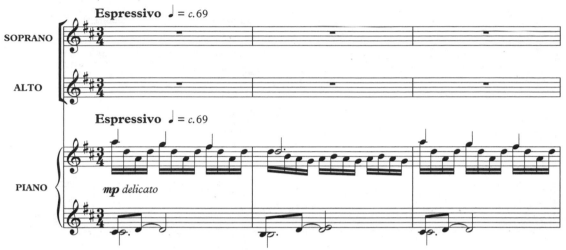

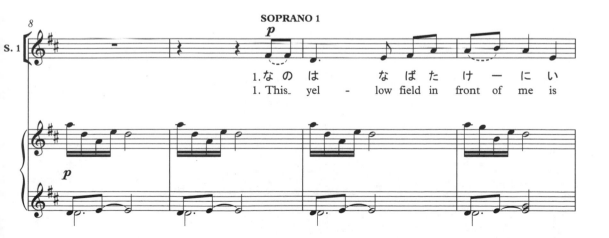

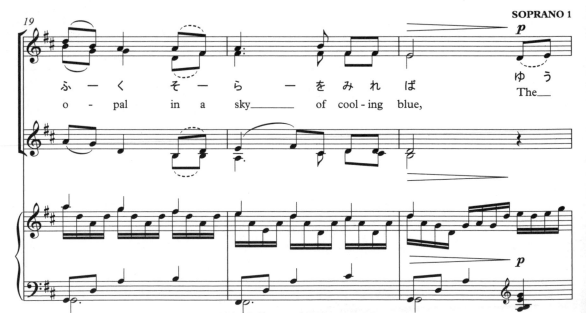

18 Oborozukiyo

め ー る お ー ぼ ー ろ づ き よ
dance the moon as I did__ when I was young.

oo_____

2011年3月の東日本大震災と津波による
犠牲者の方々への追悼の為に

Furusato
故郷

Tatsuyuki Takano (1876–1947)
English version by
Charles Bennett (b. 1954)

TEIICHI OKANO (1878–1941)
arr. BOB CHILCOTT (b. 1955)

1. う さ ぎ お い し か の や ま こ ぶ な
1. Dream-ing I see the green moun-tains a-gain, Ri-vers so

Momiji
紅葉

Tatsuyki Takano (1876–1947)
English version by
Charles Bennett (b. 1954)

TEIICHI OKANO (1878–1941)
arr. BOB CHILCOTT (b. 1955)

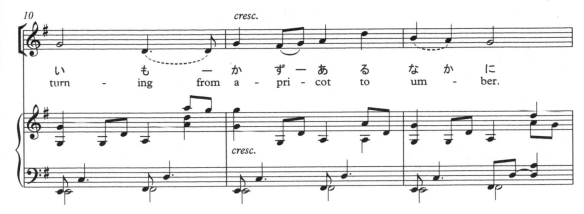

す　そ—も　よ　う　—
shi - ver and glim - mer.

2. た　に　の　な　が
2. Drift - ing___ on the

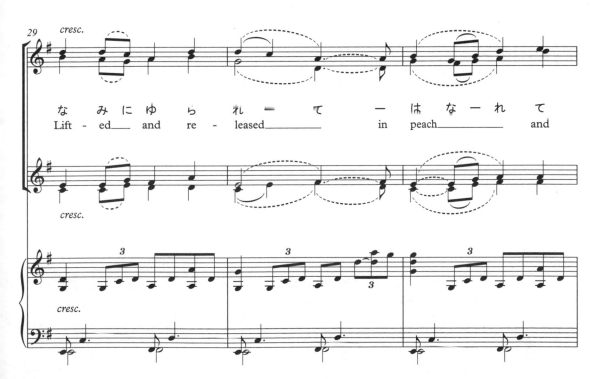

にーも　　おるーにしき　ー
leaves,_____　leaves_____ on the wa - ter,

おるーにしき　　　ー
Au-tumn is paint-ing　leaves._____

Processed in England by Enigma Music Production Services, Amersham, Bucks.
Printed in England by Halstan & Co. Ltd, Amersham, Bucks.

詩

砂山

作詞: 北原白秋
作曲: 中山晋平

一、　海は荒海
　　　向うは佐渡よ
　　　すずめなけなけ
　　　もう日は暮れた
　　　みんな呼べ呼べ
　　　お星さま出たぞ

二、　暮れりゃ砂山
　　　汐鳴りばかり
　　　すずめちりちり
　　　又風荒れる
　　　みんなちりちり
　　　もう誰も見えぬ

三、　かえろかえろよ
　　　ぐみ原わけて
　　　すずめさよなら
　　　さよならあした
　　　海よさよなら
　　　さよならあした

村祭

文部省唱歌

一、　村の鎮守の　神様の
　　　今日はめでたい　御祭日
　　　ドンドンヒャララ
　　　ドンヒャララ
　　　ドンドンヒャララ
　　　ドンヒャララ
　　　朝から聞こえる　笛太鼓

二、　年も豊年　満作で
　　　村は総出の　大祭
　　　ドンドンヒャララ
　　　ドンヒャララ
　　　ドンドンヒャララ
　　　ドンヒャララ
　　　夜まで賑う　宮の森

三、　稔の秋に　神様の
　　　めぐみたたえる　村祭
　　　ドンドンヒャララ
　　　ドンヒャララ
　　　ドンドンヒャララ
　　　ドンヒャララ
　　　聞いても心が　勇み立つ

おぼろ月夜

作詞: 高野辰之
作曲: 岡野貞一

一、　　菜の花畑に　入日薄れ
　　　　見渡す山の端　霞深し
　　　　春風そよ吹く　空を見れば
　　　　夕月かかりて　匂い淡し

二、　　里わの火影も　森の色も
　　　　田中の小道を　辿る人も
　　　　蛙の鳴く音も　鐘の音も
　　　　さながら霞める　おぼろ月夜

故郷

作詞: 高野辰之
作曲: 岡野貞一

一、　　兎おいし　かの山
　　　　小鮒釣りし　かの川
　　　　夢は今も　めぐりて
　　　　忘れがたき　故郷

二、　　如何にいます　父母
　　　　恙なしや　友がき
　　　　雨に風に　つけても
　　　　思い出ずる　故郷

三、　　志を　はたして
　　　　いつの日にか　帰らん
　　　　山は青き　故郷
　　　　水は清き　故郷

紅葉

作詞: 高野辰之
作曲: 岡野貞一

一、　　秋の夕日に　照る山紅葉
　　　　こいもうすいも　かずあるなかに
　　　　松をいろどる　かえでやつたは
　　　　山のふもとの　すそもよう

二、　　谷の流れに　散り浮く紅葉
　　　　波にゆられて　はなれてよって
　　　　赤や黄いろの　色さまざまに
　　　　水の上にも　織る錦